EXCITEMENT FOR PROVEN PRINCIPLES

It has taken Pastor Gary a life-time to write *Proven Principles: To Awaken and Ignite the Leader Inside You*.

In reading his book, it became very clear that these principles are not based on the same old secular leadership punch list of things to do and not to do. Instead, this work is sacred. It clearly points to a total dependency on the Holy Spirit.

As the President of *Cornerstone Television*, I had the wonderful privilege of serving with Pastor Gary for many years on our Board of Directors. He brought to our ministry great wisdom, understanding, knowledge, and joy. He is divinely prepared to share from his lifelong experience of following Jesus.

This book isn't just for established leaders, it is for everyone who desires to serve God and fulfill His purposes. *Proven Principles* makes very clear that powerful leadership cannot be learned, it must be demonstrated. It is filled with scriptural insight, clear instruction, and spiritual revelation.

I highly recommend that you read this book and apply its *Proven Principles* to your everyday walk with Jesus! He will amaze you!

Don Black
Founder
Finishing Strong Coaching

I have known Pastor Gary for over 20 years. For many years he would host a Pastor's Conference at my church in Iquitos, Peru. When we would announce to our association that Pastor Gary was coming for a three-day conference, more than 200 pastors would attend to hear what this man of God had to say. Many pastors and leaders in our area have been blessed and continue to be blessed by Pastor Gary. He is a pastor to pastors.

I am excited for you to read his book. I know that you will be encouraged and will gain wisdom from this man of God.

Ramon Sahuarico
Pastor
Philadelphia Church, Iquitos, Peru

I am sure you've heard the saying, "He is one of a kind." Gary gives that statement legitimacy. I've known this man for over 50 years and he is for real. So is the anointing that God has placed on him and I might add, remains on him. In his home, in the pulpit, and wherever you meet him, he is bigger than life. God has place a uniqueness on Gary as you will see as you read through the pages of this book. He is truly a man with a word in due season. The words tucked away in this writing are genuinely like "apples of gold in pictures of silver."

Lester S. Hall
Founder & CEO
New Life Church, Billings, MT

In life there are fixed and certain principles that govern our lives.

Gravity. What goes up, will always come down.

Sowing and reaping. "While the earth remains, seedtime and harvest, cold and heat, summer and winter, day and night, shall not cease."

All principles, set in place by the wisdom of God.

What difference does leadership make? Look around, a mighty nation can stumble because of lack of leadership. Yet, any astute observer would know that if the correct principles were put in place, a transformation would take place, and our nation would revive.

I've known Gary Tustin for decades. I watched him create a growing, successful church in a town that had been judged to be in decline. Principles trump circumstances every time.

My mother told me as I grew, "Emulate leaders who are successful, it will accelerate your own success." It was true fifty years ago, it is true today.

Avail yourself of a successful man, who has in this new book laid out for you a clear path, "a lamp unto your feet," if you will, that can, if followed, get you to your destiny on a more direct road!

Thank you, Gary, for a lifetime of principled living, and for taking time to gather your lifetime of wisdom and sharing it with us in *Proven Principles: To Awaken and Ignite the Leader Inside You!*

Philip Cameron
Founder
The Orphans Hands Ministry

As a pastor of more than 40 years, and leadership professor at Geneva College and Point Park University for more than 25 years, it brings me great joy to see that you have written *Proven Principles*. I have watched and conversed with you over the decades and know that you have walked the talk. These principles will help both the pastor who has been on this journey for a while, and will equally help and sure up the path for those aspiring leaders about to embark on God's journey through the Word of God.

Proven Principles is a much needed read and reread for anyone serious about biblical leadership.

Mitchel Nickols, Ph.D.
Author, Professor, Mentor, and
Church and Organizational Consultant

There are many leaders who live for their own personal gain or recognition, and then you have those like Pastor Gary who give their lives to raise up others as leaders. I was one of those that Pastor Gary believed in and invested in as a young man just starting out in pastoral ministry. This book is a culmination of his life impartation to raise up the next generation of godly leadership.

Craig Nanna
Pastor
Life Church, Reading, PA

As I walked through the streets of Punta Piedra, a poverty-stricken suburb of Lima Peru, I thought of Little Lambs of Lima, a thriving ministry meeting the needs, both spiritual and physical, of the members of that community. They were our hosts as we stayed at their beautiful facility that houses a church, school, bakery, auditorium and apartments. All of it on land that used to be just an empty lot. Through the vision, faith, and leadership of Gary Tustin, as he was led by the Holy Spirit, this kingdom ministry was established.

Pastor Gary has now put those hard-fought and hard-learned lessons into a book of wisdom. *Proven Principles: To Awaken and Ignite the Leader Inside You* will do just that: Awaken the gifts and callings that God has placed inside of each child of God. If followed, the reader will find himself establishing the kingdom of God in the place to which he is called, just as Pastor Gary has done in Johnstown, PA and Lima, Peru.

But watch out! Kingdom work comes at a cost. As Pastor Gary lets us know, "A leader cannot lead people where he's never been." Gary Tustin has been there. Are we willing to follow?

Tom Hollis
COO
Cornerstone Television Network

This book, *Proven Principles*, is for anyone who is a leader or aspires to be a leader. Pastor Gary has shared his heart to help others move up the ladder of leadership. The chapters are full of words of inspiration and nuggets of wisdom, such as: "When you are at your lowest place, give God your highest praise!" I believe this book is life-changing for everyone who reads it and applies the principles.

Joseph (Bud) Walls
Pastor
New Life Church, New Florence, PA

Pastor Gary Tustin, more affectionately known as Pastor Gary, has been a lifelong friend and colleague. His more than fifty years of distinguished ministry has produced outstanding congregations and leaders. He is indeed a pastor's pastor.

He is one of the most gifted motivators I know, with unique insights for pastoral leadership development and congregational care. When you finish reading his outstanding book—containing biblical principles that work—you will be delighted that you did. He will give you hope and inspiration in a constantly changing world and Christian landscape.

Dr. John A. Looper
Pastor
Restoration Fellowship, Cleveland, TN

PROVEN PRINCIPLES
TO AWAKEN AND IGNITE THE LEADER INSIDE YOU

GARY L. TUSTIN

Unless otherwise noted, Scripture quotations are taken from the New King James Version. Copyright 1982 by Thomas Nelson, Inc. Used by permission. All rights reserved.

Scripture quotations marked "AMPC" are taken from the Amplified Bible Classic Version.Copyright 1954, 1958, 1962, 1964, 1965, 1987 by The Lockman Foundation. Used by permission.

Scripture quotations marked "NLT" are taken from *the Holy Bible*, New Living Translation, Copyright 1996. Used by permission of Tyndale House Publishers, Inc., Wheaton, Illinois 60189. All rights reserved.

Scripture quotations marked "NIV" are taken from THE HOLY BIBLE, NEW INTERNATIONAL VERSION, NIV, Copyright 1973, 1978, 1984 by International Bible Society. Used by permission.

Italics not included in the versions cited have been added by the author for emphasis.

Proven Principles to Awaken and Ignite the Leader Inside You

ISBN 979-8-218-04354-4

Copyright © 2022 by Gary L. Tustin

Published by Writing Momentum LLC in conjunction with Greater Johnstown Christian Fellowship

Cover design, print and ebook formatting by Writing Momentum LLC

All rights reserved.

No part of this book may be reproduced in any form or by any electronic or mechanical means, including information storage and retrieval systems, without written permission from the author, except for the use of brief quotations in a book review.

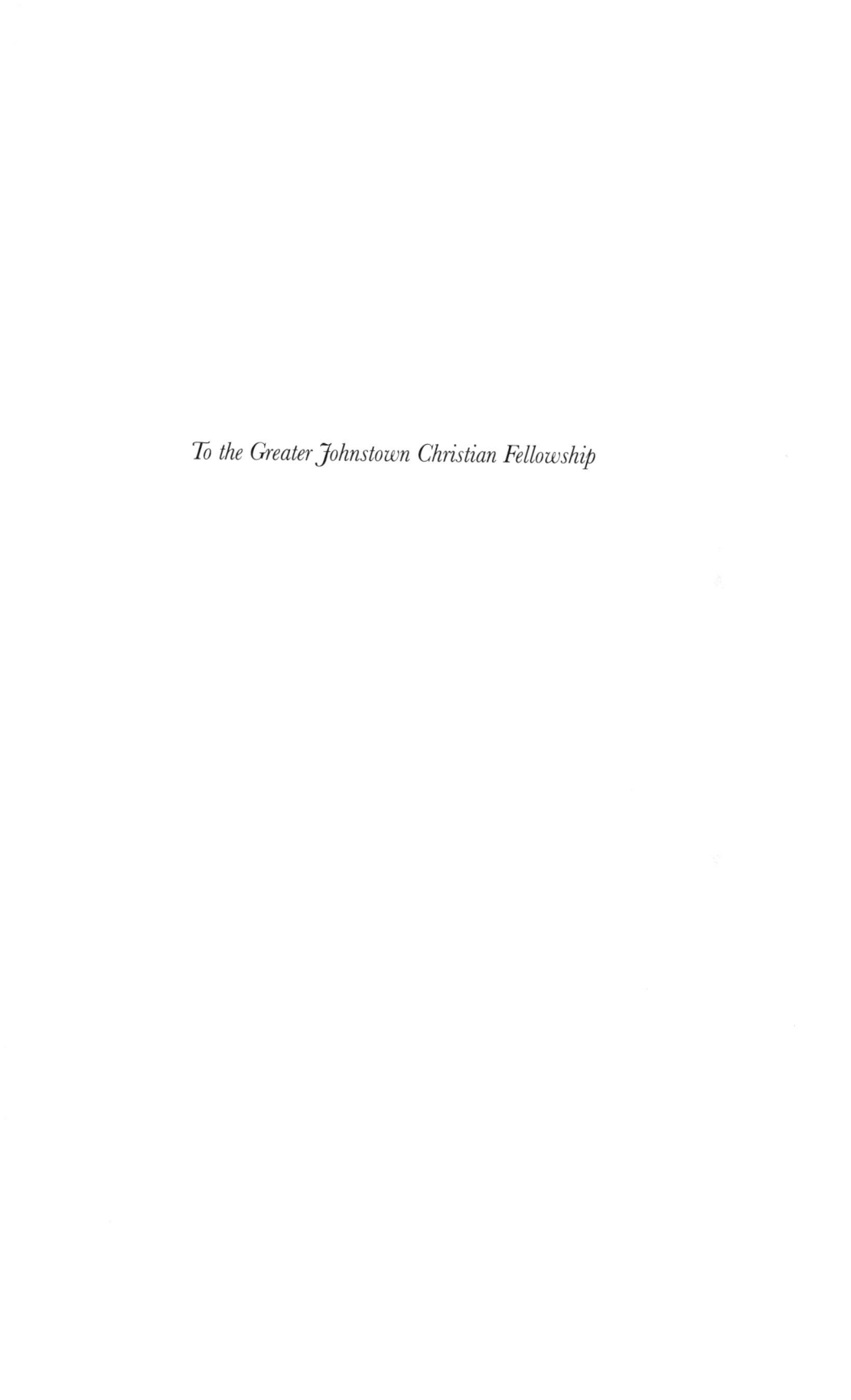

To the Greater Johnstown Christian Fellowship

CONTENTS

Foreword	xiii
Introduction	xv
1. The Principle of the Presence	1
2. The Principle of The Word	7
3. The Principle of Vision	13
4. The Principle of Faith	19
5. The Principle of Victory	25
6. The Principle of Praise	31
7. The Principle of Positive Confrontation	37
8. The Principle of Influence	43
9. The Principle of Action	49
10. The Principle of E.D.G.E	55
Leaders Who Stand Out!	61
About the Author	65

FOREWORD

Pastor Gary L. Tustin has not only been my pastor for nearly 40 years, but he has also been my spiritual dad in ministry for almost 30 years. In that time, he has taught me how to have a strong work ethic and the importance of a deep love for others. But above all, he has challenged me to passionately study the Bible daily and to wholly follow the Lord—loving Him with all my heart, soul, strength, and mind. These qualities were always put on full display by Pastor Gary, and they spoke a very loud message in my life…one that continues to this day.

The book you are about to read is as real as real gets. The principles shared are a result of more than 50 years of full-time ministry. They are proven and they work! Over the past several months, I have found myself returning to them over and over again as a source of inspiration and encouragement.

These *Proven Principles* have been effective gauges in my personal life and ministry. I've not only realized how far I've come in my

FOREWORD

leadership abilities, but I am also lovingly reminded that I've not yet arrived. There is still so much left to learn!

My pastor has written this book from a heart of love and belief in the next generation of ministry leaders. I am confident that you will be greatly blessed. You will be challenged. You will be stretched. And of this one thing I am certain: With this book, you will be taken to a higher level of leadership.

James L. Gay
Pastor, Greater Johnstown Christian Fellowship

INTRODUCTION

Then the Lord answered me and said:
"Write the vision and make it plain on tablets,
That he may run who reads it. For the vision is yet for an
  appointed time; But at the end it will speak, and it will
  not lie. Though it tarries, wait for it;
Because it will surely come, it will not tarry."

HABAKKUK 2:2-3

What began as a Bible Study of 16 members in 1982 has become a vibrant church of nearly 1,100 affiliates in 40 years, but that's not really our story. Our story is what we have come through in *becoming* who we are today and the leadership principles that we have learned in the process.

First and foremost, I want to give praise to God for what He has accomplished. **Look what the Lord has done!** What once

INTRODUCTION

was a vision in my spirit and a dream of a community has become the Greater Johnstown Christian Fellowship.

During a recent trip in what I thought was a farewell tour of our missionary compound in Lima, Peru, something happened that continued to burn inside of me. No one there at the time knew that I was considering this visit as my last. Just as I was preparing to leave to come back home, a group of pastors came to me and said, "Papa, we need what God has given you. Please, Papa, we need you!"

Over the past several months, I have found myself saying, "I want to die empty." At first, I really didn't know what I was saying, but now I am seeing this dream become a reality.

 A dream written down becomes a goal. A goal broken down into steps becomes a plan. A plan backed by action becomes a reality!

God is turning my talk into a walk. I want to invite you to walk with me as we journey through ten proven leadership principles that have changed my life. Each principle inspired me to change from being a good manager to becoming an effective leader.

Proven Principles is just that, principles that have been proven! This is not a book of methods because methods do change. This is a collection of principles that *never* change. It is so important to distinguish between methods and principles. Leaders who place more emphasis on methods than principles are headed for trouble. Alfred Lord Tennyson wrote, "Methods are many, principles are few. Methods will change, principles never do."

INTRODUCTION

Proven Principles will introduce you to unchangeable principles along with scriptural support in hope that they will be a seed meant to ignite further study and development. These proven principles can be applied to help you in every area of your life—personal, family, church life, and business. They are "under the sun" values meant to awaken the leader inside of you. When that happens, you are then ready to awaken leaders around you!

Principles never change, they will always work, if you do! Remember you cannot lead someone to a place where you've never been. This book is meant not only to develop you, but others as well. If you want to add to your church, attract followers. If you want to multiply your church, develop leaders.

Investing in your success,
Pastor Gary L. Tustin

CHAPTER 1
THE PRINCIPLE OF THE PRESENCE

Then he said to Him, "If Your Presence does not go with us, do not bring us up from here."

EXODUS 33:15

THE CALL WAS SIMPLE.

"Moses, Depart and *go up* from here, you and the people whom you brought out of the land of Egypt" (Exodus 33:1). **This is what this study is all about—leading people up!**

It was no coincidence that before God called Moses to lead the people up that Moses would first have an encounter with God and be called up to Mount Sinai. Here it is: "The Lord said to Moses, '*Come up* to Me on the mountain and be there' ... and Moses *went up*" (Exodus 24:12-13). Forty days of glory in the presence of God!

A leader cannot lead people to where he's never been! When Moses returned from the mountain, the presence of God shone on his face (Exodus 34:29). This is a powerful leadership principle: God wanted Israel to follow a leader who had a visible witness of the presence of God.

 A leader cannot lead people to where he's never been!

After the death of Moses, God told Joshua, "This day I will begin to exalt you in the sight of all Israel, that they may know that as I was with Moses, so shall I be with you" (Joshua 3:7).

The witness of the presence of God in a leader's life always was and always will be a leadership principle. Why? God does not want His people to follow a person but rather He wanted them to follow His presence *in* that person. This is clearly witnessed in the life of Paul also. In 1 Corinthians 11:1, He reminded the Church, "Imitate me, just as I also imitate Christ." In other words, "Follow me as I follow Christ."

You may be there right now, and God has called you to lead your family, your friends, your church *up* yet you keep thinking, *But, God, how can I do this?* God's answer to Moses, to Joshua, to Paul and to you is the same, "My presence will go with you" (Exodus 33:14). You see, **principles never change.** Without God's presence whatever He has called you to do will never happen. **In God's presence are all the resources you need to lead people up.** As David said, "In Your Presence is fullness of joy" (Psalm 16:11). Nothing can lift people up as can the joy of the Lord.

PROVEN PRINCIPLES

For He dwells with you and will be in you.

JOHN 14:17

God's presence took on a new dimension on the Day of Pentecost (Acts 2:1-4). Prior to that day, God's Presence came *upon* those who were called to fulfill His purpose. Now, after Pentecost, everything changed, God's presence was not only *with* them, but His presence was also *in* them!

Jesus commissioned His disciples to "Go therefore and make disciples of all the nations" (Matthew 28:19). This is the Great Commission, but His last commission to His disciples was not to *go,* but rather to *wait:* "Wait until you are endued with power from on high" (Luke 24:49).

The presence of God became visible as Peter's fear was turned into faith. Even the Sanhedrin Council "perceived that they had been with Jesus" (Acts 4:13). What a difference the presence of God can make!

So that times of refreshing may come from the Presence of the Lord.

ACTS 3:19

Don't read that verse too fast. Did you get it? "Times of refreshing" means that being filled the Holy Spirit is not just a one-time experience. The same group of followers who were filled on the Day of Pentecost were filled again: "And when they had prayed, the place where they were assembled together was shaken; and they were all filled with the Holy Spirit, and they spoke the word of God with boldness" (Acts 4:31).

The promise of Pentecost continues to be necessary for ministry. "For the promise is to you and to your children and to all who are afar off, as many as the Lord our God will call" (Acts 2:39).

May the words of our Lord be a guiding light for all who accept His call into leadership: "Wait until you are endued with power from on high." Why? Paul gives us the answer: "that no flesh should glory in His Presence" (1 Corinthians 1:29).

 Hey Leader, if you've got it, God gave it!

PROVEN PRINCIPLES

- Are you trying to lead people through your personality or by the presence of God?

- Is God speaking to you, inviting you to come into His presence?

- Is God inviting you to times of refreshing?

- Have you been relying on your own experience instead of His presence?

NOTES

_____

_____

_____

_____

_____

CHAPTER 2
THE PRINCIPLE OF THE WORD

Revive me according to Your Word.

PSALM 119:25

IT IS the responsibility of the leader to connect the Word of God with the presence of God in order to be equipped to lead the people of God. Paul told Timothy, "All Scripture is given by the inspiration of God ... that the man of God may be complete ... equipped for every good work" (2 Timothy 3:16-17).

> **Before a leader can make the Word exciting for others, it must first excite the leader!**

The Word is given by the inspiration of God and unless it is received with the same inspiration, it will remain just words. The *Quarterly Review, Volume 109-1861* wrote, "All Scripture is inspired by God, yet the time will come when educated men will make them as words again" (paraphrased).

While we read for *information,* we must pray for *revelation!* Paul's prayer for the Church in Ephesus was that God would give them "the Spirit of wisdom and revelation" (Ephesians 1:17). The Word of God mixed with the presence of God will bring change in the lives of the people of God. The Word of God was not only written for *information;* it was written for *transformation.*

The Word gives the leader INFORMATION which becomes INSPIRATION that we may become the CONTINUAL INCARNATION which is, "Christ in you, the hope of glory" (Colossians 1:27). As leaders, our goal is to offer that hope to the hopeless, just as Paul wrote, "It is no longer I who lives, but Christ who lives in me" (Galatians 2:20).

When the Word of God and the presence of God come together inside of us, ministry happens! "But if our gospel is veiled, it is veiled to those who are perishing" (2 Corinthians 4:3).

> *I have treasured the words of His mouth more than my necessary food.*
>
> JOB 23:12

Wow! What a description of Job's love for God's words. It was the reason for his patience and integrity. "In all this Job did not sin" (Job 1:22). He lost everything except his integrity, even after his wife told him to "curse God and die" (Job 2:9). How did he do this? The answer: "Thy Word have I hid in my heart that I may not sin against You" (Psalm 119:11).

The words of God meant more to Job than the words of his wife. While Job loved her, he loved God's Word more, and it paid off!

In the last chapter of his book, we read, "Indeed, the Lord gave Job twice as much as he had before" (Job 42:10). I guess you could say Job received double for his trouble, all because of his love for the Word!

Psalm 119 is the longest chapter in the Bible because it is about the greatest book in the world—the Word of God. We are reminded that, "The entrance of Your words gives light" (v. 130); "The entirety of Your word is truth" (v. 160); "Forever, O Lord, Your word is settled in heaven" (v. 89). The Word cannot be improved upon; it is settled in heaven.

A caution going forward, we need to be reminded that in these last days there will come those who "exchanged the truth of God for the lie" (Romans 1:25). When the Word is changed, we lose our moral compass. The Word is the indispensable center, "but My words will by no means pass away" (Matthew 24:35).

When Jesus began His earthly ministry, He gave us a powerful principle of the Word. After He fasted for forty days and nights, Jesus was tempted in three different areas of life that we are faced with on a daily basis: "the lust of the flesh, the lust of the eyes, and the pride of life" (1 John 2:16). Remember this: Fasting gives us victory over temptation, but the Word is a weapon against deception!

With each temptation Jesus responded by saying, "It is written" (Matthew 4:4,7,10). Did you catch that? God's Word is the answer to every single temptation we will ever face in this life. This is worth repeating: **Fasting gives us victory over temptation, but the Word is a weapon against deception!**

Let the Word be like a fire and a hammer to you. The prophet Jeremiah reminds us, "His word was in my heart like a *burning fire* shut up in my bones." (Jeremiah 20:9) and "Is not My word like a *fire* ... and like a *hammer* that breaks the rock in pieces" (Jeremiah 23:29)?

As we conclude, I would love to share something that Charles Spurgeon said that has made an impact in my life. May it be an encouragement to you too. "I owe more to the fire, and the hammer, and the file, than to anything else in my Lord's workshop."

 One final word for you to keep central in your leadership journey: "Preach the Word!" (2 Timothy 4:2)

PROVEN PRINCIPLES

- Do you read the Word for information without praying for revelation?

- Do you need to increase your love of God's Word?

- How are you using God's Word as a weapon against deception?

- How has the Word been like a fire to you? How about a hammer? Is the Word your indispensable center?

NOTES

_____

_____

_____

_____

_____

_____

CHAPTER 3
THE PRINCIPLE OF VISION

Where there is no vision, the people perish.

PROVERBS 29:18, KJV

SOLOMON SAID, "Where there is no vision, the people perish" (Proverbs 29:18, KJV). Why? Vision looks forward, routine and tradition looks backward. Without vision life is a constant rerun, and that's a horrible rut to be in. God created us to advance, not retreat. He reminded Israel that He would give them "a future and a hope" (Jeremiah 29:11).

> **Vision is seeing what God is saying!**

Vision is not a rerun, it's not boring, it can sometimes feel threatening because vision will take us to a place that we have never been before. Vision requires God's participation. When individuals, churches, or even businesses are *between chapters*, the past can seem attractive, the present comfortable, and the future fearful, but when it's His vision, He will be the provision.

Joshua came to a place of *between chapters* in Joshua 3. For three days he was with God receiving instruction on how to lead Israel across the Jordan. God told Joshua, "You have not passed this way before" (v. 4). This was not a rerun of the Red Sea crossing, this was a *now* word for a *new* time. Don't rely on past experiences. God is never predictable!

Israel crossed the Red Sea on dry ground (Exodus 14:29). Now, at the Jordan as the priests put their feet in the water, the ground became dry "in the midst of the Jordan" and all Israel crossed (v. 15, 17). Thank God for vision!

Joshua CAUGHT the vision to cross over Jordan, then he waited three days for God to CLARIFY the vision before he CAST the vision to the Israelites. Wow, did you notice the progression?

Leadership is a journey, not a destination. God's vision is always developing. Throughout the Bible when God was guiding His people, He would often say to them, "I will show you." Our lives are not reruns. We cannot rely on our past experiences. God is speaking the same words to us today, "I will show you."

VISION KEEPS US CONNECTED TO GOD!

God spoke to Moses about his next step through a vision. So in Exodus 24 we read that Moses ascends to Mount Sinai and stays there for forty days. I like this word, "Then the Lord said to Moses, 'Come up to Me on the mountain and *be there*'" (Exodus 24:12). God's invitation is still the same: "Come up to Me and be there!"

Many visions never fully develop because often we will come into God's presence to catch the vision, but we fail to stay in His presence for God to clarify the vision. It is important to understand that when we seek God for vision, **don't be in a hurry and remove all distractions**.

God said to Moses, "Make Me a sanctuary that I may dwell with them" (Exodus 25:8). Moses was then given a vision from God on how to accomplish the task. When the vision was completed, Scripture tells us, "Moses *finished* the work" (Exodus 40:33). This particular part of the vision was finished, but Moses wasn't, there was still more for him to do.

Moses caught and God clarified the vision. After 40 days, Moses cast the vision to God's people. We enter God's presence to catch the vision, then we must allow God to clarify the vision before we are ever able to cast the vision. Remember, **when God gives vision, He will not show you the whole staircase, only the next step!**

God spoke to Nehemiah through a *burden*. Nehemiah learned that the walls that surrounded Jerusalem were broken down. So for three months he prayed for God to give him a vision on how to rebuild the walls.

God gave the vision and Nehemiah was given permission to return to Jerusalem and rebuild. Watch this, "So the wall was finished ... in fifty-two days" (Nehemiah 6:15). This particular part of the vision was finished, but Nehemiah wasn't, there was still more for him to do.

Once again in each account, the vision was given, steps were taken, and that part of the vision was completed, but Moses and

Nehemiah had more to do. This is huge! When we are between chapters, it becomes so tempting to just focus on celebrating our past accomplishment that we close ourselves off to the next chapter. **Life is in vision, not in celebration**. Do you need a spiritual lift? Pray for vision.

> *The path of the just is as the shining light, that shineth more and more unto the perfect day.*
>
> PROVERBS 4:18, KJV

God will guide us until Jesus returns! We are not called to do *everything*; we are called to do *something*. There is a purpose that will bring about the greatest joy in our lives when we discover it. Do you remember the opening verse? "Where there is no vision, the people perish." There is no substitute for vision.

Think about this: **Your occupation is your decision; your vocation is your discovery.** God has placed a purpose inside of you, and you are perfectly designed for it.

Paul wrote, "Walk in a manner worthy of the vocation wherein you are called" (Ephesians, 4:1, KJV). People who are perishing are those who are not walking in their vocation. Their main concern is their occupation.

A successful career cannot bring about personal fulfillment unless it is connected to your vocation. Here it is, your occupation supports your vocation. It's your vocation not occupation that gets you up in the morning.

PROVEN PRINCIPLES

Life is in your vocation because vision is seeing what God is saying and His words are life. Vision makes the difference! Once you've experienced significance, success will never satisfy!

GARY L. TUSTIN

IGNITORS

- Has God given you a vision for your future?

- Are you struggling with how your vision can happen?

- Are you spending enough time in God's presence for Him to clarify your vision?

- Is your life a continual rerun?

- Are you relying too much on your experience and not enough on God's provision?

- Are you giving more attention to your occupation than you are to your vocation?

NOTES

CHAPTER 4
THE PRINCIPLE OF FAITH

Jesus answered and said to them, "Have faith in God."

MARK 11:22

SCRIPTURE DECLARES, "For by grace you have been saved through faith" (Ephesians 2:8), and "But without faith it is impossible to please Him" (Hebrews 11:6). Faith is necessary for our conversion and completion! **God would not require anything from us unless He would provide for us.** So here's what He has done, "God has dealt to each one the *measure* of faith" (Romans 12:3, KJV). God gives us the faith to be saved, then it is up to each individual to further develop their measure of faith.

Faith is a bridge between where I am and where He is taking me!

In the New Testament there are no less than six levels of faith:

1. Little Faith (Matthew 6:30)
2. Great Faith (Matthew 8:10)
3. No Faith (Mark 4:40)
4. Full of Faith (Acts 6:8)
5. Weak Faith (Romans 4:19)
6. Empty Faith (1 Corinthians 15:54)

All the various levels of faith began as the measure of faith.

Jesus likened faith to a mustard seed. A mustard seed is the smallest of seeds, yet it grows and becomes greater than all herbs (Mark 4:31). Faith is also like a spiritual muscle that increases with use or decreases with no use. The Bible is filled with examples of how faith is developed.

James connects faith with trials (James 1:2-3), and Peter associates trials with genuine faith (1 Peter 1:7). Faith does not flourish in a five-star hotel, it is like film that is developed in the dark. So don't downgrade your dream to match your history, upgrade your faith to match your destiny.

In James 1:26 we read that, "faith without works is dead." Faith isn't just flexing a spiritual muscle in hopes that it will grow. Faith must be mixed with works.

> *But the Word which they heard did not profit them, not being mixed with faith.*
>
> HEBREWS 4:2

The Jews *believed* that God would send the Messiah, they just didn't have *faith* that Jesus was the Promised One. They failed to mix their belief with faith. Here's how belief and faith connect.

Belief says, "God can," and faith says, "God will." Do you see the difference? As a leader, we are called upon to turn believers into receivers. Faith is a seed that grows in an environment of need.

In Mark 2, a paralyzed man was carried on a bed by four friends to see Jesus. The crowd who gathered around Jesus was so large that these men could not enter the house where Jesus was staying. So they uncovered the roof and lowered their friend so he could be healed.

Notice what happens next, "When Jesus saw their faith," this man's sins were forgiven (v. 5). He was told by Jesus to rise up and walk ... and he did! This happened because Jesus saw *their* faith.

As a leader, we will be called upon to have faith for the faithless. This was the setting for the apostles when they were with Jesus. They said to Him, "Lord, increase our faith" (Luke 17:5).

We, too, can have increased faith. Scripture reminds us, "But you, beloved, building yourselves up on your most holy faith, praying in the Holy Spirit" (Jude 20). Don't be surprised what happens next when you ask for increased faith. Let's take a look at the life of Habakkuk.

Habakkuk prayed and God delayed His answer. We don't know for sure how long the answer was delayed, but we do know that when the answer came, Habakkuk wasn't thrilled. What was God doing? He was building Habakkuk's faith. Did it work? Yes, it did! Habakkuk declared, "the just shall live by faith" (Habakkuk 2:4).

God used delays and disappointments to develop Habakkuk's faith. His faith grew so much that he wrote a profound hymn of faith at the end of his book (Habakkuk 3:17-19). It's worth the read.

> **Sometimes we have to go through the worst before we get to God's best!**

A quick word about delays. Sometimes God will delay so that the evil that lies ahead of us will pass before we get to where we need to be. This is one of the ways that God protects us. When God makes us wait, He has our development and protection in mind. Sometimes we have to go through the worst before we get to God's best.

Throughout the gospels of Matthew, Mark, and Luke, Jesus spoke often in parables to His disciples about developing faith. When the disciples faced a furious storm, faith came to the front and center. Jesus responded to them by saying, "You of little faith, why are you so afraid?" (Matthew 8:26); "Do you still have no faith?" (Mark 4:40); and "Where is your faith" (Luke 8:25)?

The disciples were concerned about their DEATH in the storm, Jesus was concerned about their DEVELOPMENT of faith in the storm.

> **Fear is a reaction; Faith is a decision!**

Leader, don't be guilty of misrepresenting faith. Faith is not about everything turning out okay but about being okay no matter how things turn out!

IGNITORS

- Where is your level of faith?

- How have you been daily developing your faith?

- Can you witness continual growth in your faith?

- If you believe God *can*, do you need increased faith to believe that God *will?*

- Do you need increased faith so that you have faith for others?

NOTES

_____
_____
_____
_____
_____

CHAPTER 5
THE PRINCIPLE OF VICTORY

And this is the victory ... our faith.

1 JOHN 5:4

As a leader and follower of Jesus Christ, we do not *go to* victory, we *come from* victory. Wow! Let that word sink deep in your spirit. Paul wrote, "But thanks be to God, who gives the victory through our Lord Jesus Christ" (1 Corinthians 15:57). Our victory comes through the death and resurrection of Jesus.

> **We do not go to victory, we come from victory!**

Here it is, "Looking unto Jesus, the author and finisher of our faith, who for the *joy* that was *set* before Him endured the cross, despising the shame, and has sat down at the right hand of the throne of God" (Hebrews 12:2). How could Jesus face the shame and the pain on the cross and consider it joy? The answer is found in this verse: "Who for the joy that was set before Him." Jesus set His focus forward on the resurrection.

"Now thanks be to God who *always* leads us in triumph in Christ" (2 Corinthians 2:14). This is how we come from a place of victory. Paul reminded the Church, "Let this mind be in you which was also in Christ Jesus" (Philippians 2:5). The key to this verse is "let." We already have victory regardless of what happens. Victory is in an inside job before it becomes visible.

Jesus *set* the joy before Him, then He was able to face the shame and endure the pain on the cross. Think about it: **All sorrow has a positive ending through Christ Jesus!** "Weeping may endure for a night, but joy comes in the morning" (Psalm 30:5). "Many are the afflictions of the righteous, but the Lord delivers them out of them all" (Psalm 34:19).

> **Rather than speaking words that describe our situation, we speak words that can change our situation!**

Thinking faith thoughts and speaking faith words will lead the heart out of defeat and into victory! Rather than speaking words that describe our situation, we speak words that can change our situation. Did you get that? We come from victory to victory. Having the mind of Christ, we can see victory even before it is realized. From our hearts, our mouths speak and with the "mind of Christ," we speak from a position of victory, not defeat.

Death and life are in the power of the tongue.

PROVERBS 18:21

Let's take a look at David's prayer from a cave. "Refuge has failed me; no one cares for my soul, I cried to You, O Lord; I said, 'You are my refuge ... the righteous shall surround me'" (Psalm 142:4-5,7). Before David experienced victory, he saw himself out of the cave and rejoicing with the righteous. In Psalm 91, David wrote, "I will say of the Lord, 'He is my refuge'" (v.2).

We must take note of David's position when he wrote this, here's what he writes, "He who dwells in the secret place of the Most High shall abide under the shadow of the Almighty" (v. 1). David spoke from a position of victory even though he was in a cave with no way of escape. Jesus spoke from a position of victory, that is why He was able to consider the cross, the shame and the pain as "joy."

One more example, in 2 Kings 19, Israel was taken captive by the Assyrians. When Hezekiah, king of Judah heard the news of Israel's captivity, he "went into the house of the Lord" (v. 1). This was Hezekiah's place of victory. It was in the house of the Lord that God spoke this word through the prophet Isaiah, "Do not be afraid of the words which you have heard" (v. 6). Here's where it gets good! God said that He would cause the king of Assyria to hear a rumor, and from that rumor he would fall "by the sword in his own hand" (v. 7).

❝ Ignore the roar!

Everything changed when Hezekiah went into the house of the Lord. From this position of victory, Hezekiah, "ignored the roar!" We know that Satan "is as a roaring lion seeking whom he may devour" (1 Peter 5:8). God is calling for leaders today to lead from a position of victory. From our cave we declare these words, "You are my refuge," and ignore the roar!

Now, for the rest of the story. On a certain night, the angel of the Lord went out to the Assyrian camp and killed 185,000 men (2 Kings 19:35). What a great reminder. We may feel outnumbered and overwhelmed, but from our position of victory, we can confidently declare, "You are my refuge." Hallelujah!

IGNITORS

- How often do you find yourself going to victory rather than coming from victory?

- Do you find yourself using more negative or positive words to describe difficult situations?

- In what areas of your life do you need to "ignore the roar?"

NOTES

CHAPTER 6
THE PRINCIPLE OF PRAISE

My heart is steadfast, O God, my heart is steadfast;
I will sing and give praise.

PSALM 57:7

THE PRINCIPLE of praise must precede the PRACTICES of praise, before we receive the POWER through praise. When a statement is repeated in Scripture as seen in our opening verse, it is for the sake of emphasis. If our emphasis is on the *expressions* of praise rather than the *heart* of praise, we will not be able to experience God's promised blessings through praise.

Praise is inner health made audible!

Scripture tells us, "Keep your heart with all diligence, for out of it spring the issues of life" (Proverbs 4:23). The heart is the seat of affections. Whatever our hearts are attracted to, that is what will spring forth in our lives. The *origination* of praise must come from a heart of gratitude before it will ever reach its intended *destination*. Never confuse praise with singing. When you sing a song, that song will come to an end. When you praise with a song, you give your praise a destination, the throne room of God. In Psalm 22:3 we read that God "inhabits the praises of His people." Did you get it? God does not inhabit the singing of His people. He inhabits their praise!

One valuable key to understanding principles found in Scripture is finding its first mention, this is known as The Law of First Usage. This law helps to allow understanding of the principle's purpose throughout the entire Bible. Let's pray for understanding and revelation on the principle of praise!

The first mention of "praise" in Scripture is found in connection to the birth of Leah's fourth son, Judah. In Genesis 29, we read that Jacob married Leah due to a deceitful switch of sisters. Yes, Jacob married Leah, but he was in love with her older sister Rachel. You can understand how Leah must have felt. She was unloved by her husband. Yet, despite her rejection, God opened Leah's womb and she bore a son whom *she* named Reuben which means "God saw my affliction."

Later, she bore a second son whom *she* named Simeon, his name means "God hears." Then Leah gave birth to a third son and *she* named him, Levi, meaning "attached." Finally, she had a fourth son, *she* named him, Judah. Judah means "praise." Leah said, "Now I will praise the Lord" (Genesis 29:35).

> **Praise cannot come out of our acquaintance with God. Praise must come from our inward attachment to God!**

Did you notice that when Leah named each of her sons each name represented a healing that was taking place in her heart? Remember that praise is inner health made audible. Here's a powerful point, Leah could not praise God based on her legal attachment through marriage to Jacob, but with her heart she had to feel the connection. Praise cannot come out of our acquaintance with God, it must come from our inward attachment to God, so praise is not just an action, it's a developing reaction springing from our relationship with Jesus. Praise the Lord!

Leah's birth of Judah (praise) is a key that will unlock the door of God's promises through praise. This key is not about the method or practice of praise, but this is about the principle of praise. Methods ultimately change as is witnessed in today's culture, yet principles never change. Here is the key, in Scripture, when you come across the word "Judah," replace it with the word "praise." When you do, you will see the benefits God freely gives to us when we praise!

Let's track together as we search through Scripture God's blessings through praise.

- When Joseph shared his dreams with his brothers, they threw him into a pit out of anger. After the brothers want to kill Joseph, Judah's words spared his life and lifted him out of the pit. **When you are at your lowest place, give God your highest praise.**

- From his death bed, Jacob spoke a prophetic word that through the line of Judah would come the Lion of Judah, or Jesus (Genesis 49:9-10). People unaware of the power of praise often live in fear of the roaring lion (1 Peter 5:8), and those who know how to praise just *ignore the roar*!
- The Lord assigned Judah to dwell at the entrance of the tabernacle, "on the east side, toward the rising of the sun" (Numbers 2:3). We enter the presence of God through praise. People of praise are the first to see the rising of the Son. They look to God first in everything. "In everything give thanks" (1 Thessalonians 5:18).
- Some time after the death of Joshua, Israel asked the Lord, "Who shall be first to go up for us against the Canaanites?" He responded, "Judah shall go up" (Judges 1:1-2). Here's our key to victory: Send praise first!
- In 1 Kings 13:1 when God needed a voice, He called a man from Judah. Hallelujah! With 290 references of Judah in the prophetic books of the Bible alone, there are so many promised blessings through praise. God is calling leaders to place more emphasis on the principles of praise over the practices of praise. Remember, "God inhabits the praises of His people" so don't simply sing songs, praise the Lord!

IGNITORS

- Have I been singing songs rather than praising with a song?

- Do I find myself complaining about my challenges more often than praising in the midst of them?

- Has my personal praise become routine and less alive?

NOTES

_____

_____

_____

_____

_____

_____

_____

_____

CHAPTER 7
THE PRINCIPLE OF POSITIVE CONFRONTATION

Jesus said to His disciples, "It is impossible that no offenses should come."

LUKE 17:1

IN TURNING His followers into leaders, Jesus gave them some important advice concerning conflict. He told them in plain words, "There will be conflicts!" Isn't that exciting news? What's interesting is the meaning of the word "offenses" from our opening Scripture. Offense means "a trap." Offenses could be a set-up for a setback.

Conflict delayed is conflict multiplied!

Every offense has the potential to cause a permanent breach in a relationship. So, when an offense comes, someone must be willing to take action to close the potential breach. According to the

Scripture, we do this through *positive confrontation*. Here's a great thought: **You cannot change what you fail to confront.**

> **Confrontation is the bridge between conflict and cooperation!**

More times than not, confrontation sounds like a bad experience because it often results in a crisis, yet it is simply the act of coming together face to face to resolve a matter. Confrontation is godly and supported by Scripture. Be careful not to confuse confrontation with retaliation. Retaliation is to "return the punishment." This is ungodly and forbidden.

The main purpose of positive confrontation is to "make every effort to keep the unity of the Spirit through the bond of peace" (Ephesians 4:3, NIV). We read that this was Paul's intention in Galatians 2:11, "Now when Peter had come to Antioch, I withstood him to his face, because he was to be blamed." When the purpose of confrontation is unity and peace this, is positive confrontation and not retaliation.

Positive confrontation is a safeguard against bitterness. Bitterness is anger turned inward. When we confront positively, we put everything on the table. That keeps the offense from taking root. Offenses take root under the table and go underground. Positive confrontation makes sure that won't happen.

> **Positive confrontation keeps the offense from going underground by putting it on the table.**

The question is, should we confront every offense? Absolutely not! We pray for wisdom to know whether we should confront, when to confront, and how to confront. Solomon said, "A man's wisdom gives him patience; it is his glory to overlook an offense" (Proverbs 19:11, NIV). A key word in this verse is "an." That means choose battles wisely.

Another question that needs answered, why do leaders fail to confront? **Confronting requires courage!** Courage must come to the front and center within the call to leadership. Courage distinguishes leaders from managers. A *manager* has hope that a problem will work itself out. A *leader* has the courage to make the tough call, decisively with firmness and integrity.

Real courage is on display when a leader who is afraid to go, will go anyway. Paul said, "I'm going to Jerusalem, I don't know what to expect, I don't know the things that will happen to me ... but none of these things move me" (Acts 20:22-24). That's courage! Paul was a leader and leaders are courageous.

If you're a leader and hesitant in confronting, you're not disqualified from leadership. In the Old Testament we read that Gideon was called by God to deliver Israel from Midianite oppression. Gideon was not courageous. When God appeared to him, he was hiding from Israel's oppressors, yet God said, "The Lord is with you, you mighty man of valor" (Judges 6:12). Gideon confessed to God that he was the least of the weakest family in all Israel. But God saw something in him that Gideon hadn't seen yet. Hey leader, if God called you, courage is inside of you!

> **When God called you, He placed inside of you seeds of what you need to accomplish your call!**

When God called Joshua, He said, "Be strong and courageous" (Joshua 1:6). Moses told Israel, "Be strong and courageous." (Deuteronomy 31:15). David told Solomon, "Be strong and courageous" (1 Chronicles 28:20). Are you getting the idea? When God called you, He placed inside of you seeds of what you need to accomplish your call.

Paul reminded Timothy, "God did not give you a spirit of timidity ... but of power" (2 Timothy 1:7). So, in John 20:19, "The doors were shut where the disciples were assembled, for fear of the Jews." In Acts 4:13, "They (Jews) observed the confidence of Peter and John." Did you catch that? Peter and John were the same disciples who were confronted by the same Jews just days before. Where did this courage come from? "They were all filled with the Holy Spirit" (Acts 4:31). Challenges will bring forth courage from within. Hey leader, "Be strong and courageous."

PROVEN PRINCIPLES

IGNITORS

- Are you a good manager or an effective leader?

- Do you often allow your anger to turn inward?

- What do you need to confront with courage?

NOTES

CHAPTER 8
THE PRINCIPLE OF INFLUENCE

*Then Moses called Joshua and said unto him,
"Be strong and of good courage, for you must go
with this people ... and cause them to inherit the land."*

DEUTERONOMY 31:7

WHAT A GREAT SCRIPTURE ON INFLUENCE. Moses knew the importance of this principle, and he influenced Joshua. Now, it was Joshua's turn to learn this valuable principle. Moses said to him, "You must go with the people" before you "cause them to inherit the land." There it is. First came the CONNECTION "with," then the VISION followed the MISSION, "cause them." People will not *go* with you until you *get* with them. It's been said, "People don't care how much you know until they know how much you care."

Influence is developed daily, but not in a day!

The sole purpose of a leader is to go higher while taking others higher with him. Jesus shared a parable in Luke 14 in which He spoke an important word on relationships. The parable took place at a wedding feast when the host said to his friend, "Friend, come up higher" (v. 10). A leader is a friend who will take you higher than you were before you met him.

> **The sole purpose of a leader is to go higher while taking others higher with him!**

People are attracted to a person with passion, this is known as "action attraction." When a leader helps another discover their purpose, the connection they share is taken to a higher level. Purpose, Passion, and Pursuit. A word of caution: True leaders are not seeking affluence, rather, seeking to influence.

A common frustration among leaders occurs when they are leading but no one is following. Don't allow that frustration to intimidate you. Let it motivate you. Remember that influence is developed daily, not in a day. May this be your starting place, not your resting place.

Let's look again at Joshua's journey. Even though Scripture called Joshua a leader (Numbers 13:2), he did not have influence. Twelve spies were sent by Moses to spy out the Promised Land. After forty days, the spies returned with mixed reviews. Joshua and Caleb wanted to return and take the land at once. The remaining ten spies did not buy into their suggestion. Both men did not have influence. As a consequence, for the negative report from the ten spies, Israel was made to wander in the desert for forty years.

One of the most painful experiences we endure is when we suffer due to another's decision. How would you feel if you had to endure forty years of challenges because of the unbelief of someone else? Life during the wilderness season didn't make much sense, but God had a purpose.

In Deuteronomy 8:2,16 we read, "Remember that the Lord your God led you all the way these forty years in the wilderness, to humble you and test you … that He might test you, to do you good in the end."

Hallelujah! Satan *tempts* us to bring the *worst* out of us, but God *tests* us to bring the *best* out of us. **When you can't trace God's hand, trust His heart.** His purpose is to do you good in the end!

During this season we read that Joshua and Caleb "wholly followed the Lord" (Joshua 14:6-8). Their faithfulness increased their influence. Joshua's and Caleb's influence was needed for what was coming next in the lives of God's people. When you are going through a difficult season, stop and think, maybe God is using that time to increase your level of influence. If it worked for Joshua and Caleb, it will work for you. The enemy may be behind this, but God is going to use this!

Back to our story, next came a showdown at the Jordan River. The Jordan River was all that stood in the way of Israel possessing the Promised Land. In Joshua 3, God told Joshua, "You have not been this way before" (v. 4). This was a new place and a new time in the leadership of Joshua. He said to the people, "Sanctify yourselves, the Lord will do wonders among you" (v. 5). Israel listens to Joshua's command, the Lord does a miraculous wonder, and "all Israel crossed over on dry ground"

(v. 17). What changed? God used the wilderness wandering to increase the influence of Joshua.

> **A leader's influence must be greater than the people's resistance to progress!**

Watch this: "Everyone who was in *distress*, everyone in *debt*, and everyone who was *discontented* gathered to him (David)…and there were about 400 men" (1 Samuel 22:2). Sounds like a group of losers! Many people would have given up on them, but David didn't. Those 400 men became known as "the mighty men" of David (2 Samuel 17:8). Where the world sees a FAILURE…God gives a FUTURE!

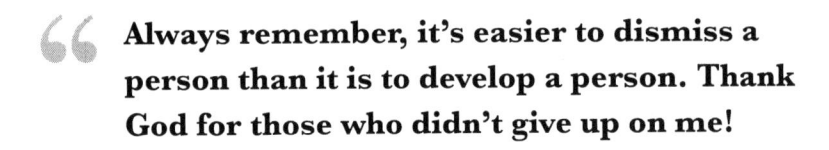

> **Always remember, it's easier to dismiss a person than it is to develop a person. Thank God for those who didn't give up on me!**

It's easy to lead people where they *want* to go. The challenge is to lead people to where they *need* to be. It is more important to influence people than it is to impress them. Leadership is not about power; it's about empowering others. A leader will influence by example, not by words. Example is not the main thing in influencing others, it's the only thing!

PROVEN PRINCIPLES

IGNITORS

- In your leadership, how have you been taking people higher?

- How do you daily develop your influence?

- In what ways do you lead people to where they need to be?

NOTES

_____
_____
_____
_____
_____
_____
_____

CHAPTER 9
THE PRINCIPLE OF ACTION

Whatever He says to you, do it.

JOHN 2:5

THIS IS a great leadership principle that will take you from "gloom to glory." The above verse of Scripture was the recorded word that Mary, the mother of Jesus, said to the servants during the wedding at Cana. "Whatever He says to you, do it." Seven words that can make a huge difference in your leadership. The longer it takes to respond to God's instruction, the more unclear it will become. Beware of procrastination and hesitation. They are two professional thieves that can get you off track and delay your dreams.

A *divine dynamic* will take place in your life when you take that next step of faith and do what God has given you to do. God's PARTICIPATION connected with your PERSPIRATION will result in His MANIFESTATION. Don't forget the key:

"Whatever He says to you, do it." Peter didn't just walk on the water; he walked on Jesus' command to "come."

Don't wait on your emotions to take action. Our emotions are wonderful servants, yet they can be terrible leaders. Paul's instruction to us is, "Be led by the Spirit" (Romans 8:14). Rather than following your feelings, follow the Word that's in your heart and confess it. Feelings follow declarations. Let's look at Deuteronomy 30:14-15:

> *But the word that is in your **mouth** and your **heart**, that you may do it. See I have set before you today life and good, death and evil.*

When God places His Word into your heart, confess it. Remember that feelings follow declarations. He has given you a set of choices and you must make a decision.

Did you know the Valley of Decision is the most visited valley in Scripture? In Joel 3:14 we read, "Multitudes, multitudes in the valley of decision."

A quick side note: When a word is repeated in the Bible, it is for the sake of emphasis. The word "multitudes" is repeated, which emphasizes the importance of this leadership principle and highlights a common problem among leaders today.

> **Action eliminates wrong options!**

The failure to make a decision is what put the Israelites in the Valley of Decision. **Indecision is a decision,** but making a decision is the first step of coming out of your valley. Your decision could shorten the distance between you and your next miracle.

Leaders are visionaries with a poorly developed sense of fear and no concept of the odds stacked against them. A leader found in Scripture who fits this definition perfectly is Esther. In the book named after her, we learn of the challenge she faced and her decision to take action. While God's name is not mentioned in the book of Esther, His hand is visible in every chapter. It's a worthwhile read.

It was nothing short of a miracle for Esther to be chosen as queen. First, she was an orphan. Next, Esther was a Jew in a Gentile kingdom. She said yes to God's call, though, and He did the rest. "Yes" is all God is wanting to hear from you, leader! Let's get back to our story. When Queen Esther learned of the king's edit to annihilate all Jews, she knew that she needed to act. Esther had to talk to the king. Here's a great thought: **A leader must know when it is necessary to be unpopular**.

To enter the king's presence without an invitation would often result in death. Queen Esther knew this, so she asked her uncle, Mordecai, to assemble the Jews to fast and pray for three days. After the three days of fasting and praying were completed, Esther made this bold statement, "I will go to the king, which is against the law, and if I perish, I perish" (Esther 4:16). Did you notice that she made her decision *before* she ever considered the consequences? There will be moments when a leader must feed on *focus* and starve *distraction*, just like Esther. Decisions determine destiny.

Esther's decision determined the destiny of the entire Jewish population. Through her courage, Jesus was born, and we can be born again. Hallelujah! Fear is a reaction, but courage is a decision. Esther did what God told her to do. **Whatever He says to you, do it.**

> **Broken focus is the leading cause for failure!**

God told Joshua, "Be strong and very courageous ... do not turn to the right hand or to the left, that you may prosper wherever you do" (Joshua 1:7). Leader, look to the prize, and look straight ahead. Problems are what a person will see when he takes his eye off the prize.

Here it is. Paul wrote in Philippians 3: "I press on" (v.12), "Reaching forward" (v. 13), and "I press toward the goal for the prize" (v. 14). When we decide this course of action, we won't turn our backs and can't be sidetracked. **Whatever He says to you, do it.**

Don't question your ability. God would never ask you do something without His participation. Don't debate it with human reasoning and by all means don't listen to what others say. JUST DO IT.

Remember this always: Without a decision there is no direction, and without direction, we stand still.

IGNITORS

- Has God put something in my heart that I must act upon?

- Have I been proactive or reactive about personal decisions?

- Have I failed to make an important decision for fear of hurting others?

- Am I one of the multitude in the Valley of Decision because I have failed to make a decision? Am I ready to make that decision?

NOTES

_____

_____

_____

_____

_____

CHAPTER 10
THE PRINCIPLE OF E.D.G.E

You are a chosen generation ... a peculiar people.

1 PETER 2:9, KJV

A LEADER IS CALLED to stand out, not blend in. One way to stand head and shoulders above the crowd is to do ordinary things in an extraordinary way with enthusiasm. This is known as *The Leader's Edge.* It's not *what* you do that sets you apart, it's *how* you do what you are called to do. **It's your attitude, not your aptitude that determines your altitude.**

> **Leaders are called to stand out, not blend in!**

One of the greatest challenges for a leader is keeping his cutting-edge sharp. When our edge is lost, our effectiveness, our distinction, and our identity are diminished. Losing our edge is not wrong. It's normal. Anything that is used will require maintenance, that's a fact. In order to maintain our edge,

Scripture makes specific references for us as leaders to be renewed.

Here it is: "Those who wait upon the Lord shall *renew* their strength" (Isaiah 40:31). What's interesting to note that the word "wait" suggests being "twisted together." Waiting on the Lord is not passive, but it's an active position of receiving. Paul reminds the church, "be transformed by the renewing of your mind" (Romans 12:2). Rather than focusing on the work of the Lord, we must first spend time with the Lord of the work. In other words, **retreat to advance!**

After Pentecost there was no coincidence that "times of refreshing" were made available to sharpen and renew believers for effective ministry (Acts 3:19). Today, there remains an open invitation for us to receive times of refreshing and renewal from the presence of God. Seeking God for renewal is not a sign of weakness. It's an act of wisdom.

In his book, *Seven Habits of Highly Successful People*, Stephen Covey writes about the seventh habit which is "sharpening the saw." He concludes his habits by stating that each habit from time to time needs to be sharpened. There it is again, keeping our cutting edge sharp is normal, natural, and necessary. Abraham Lincoln said, "Give me six hours to chop down a tree and I will spend the first four sharpening the axe."

Using the word ***E.D.G.E.*** as an acrostic, let's look at four areas where we can sharpen our edge:

E - EXCELLENCE

Scripture reminds us that God's name is excellent (Psalm 8:1). His loving kindness is excellent (Psalm 36:7). God's will is excellent. (Romans 12:1).

Before King David died, he made preparations for his son Solomon to build a house for the Lord. He said, "The house to be built for the Lord must be exceedingly magnificent" (2 Chronicles 22:15). Wow! Our God who is excellent deserves nothing less than magnificence. Paul wrote, "You are God's building" (1 Corinthians 3:9). We are God's building which is excellent, so our standard must be excellence. We are representatives of an excellent God. We've been redeemed by Jesus Christ who "did all things well" (Mark 7:34).

As Jesus did all things well, the people were astonished. Why? What He did was not normal. What Jesus did caused Him to stand out. The same will happen to you and me when we do the best we can with what we have and where we are.

D - DETERMINATION

Great things happen when a determined person and a mountain meet! Determination is not about *starting*, but it's all about *finishing*. You will stand out when you follow through with your dream until it becomes a reality. People with determination find a way or make one!

To the average person, average is awesome. Stay surrounded with people of excellence, or mediocrity will soon be acceptable.

> **Stay surrounded with people of excellence, or mediocrity will soon be acceptable!**

The Apostle Paul modeled determination in Acts 20 and Romans 8. You will read that he put *things* in its place. Here is what he wrote, "I go bound in the spirit to Jerusalem, not knowing the things that will happen to me … but none of these things move me" (Acts 20:22,24). In Romans 8 he reminds us; "All things work together for good … what shall we say to these things … yet in all these things we are more than conquerors" (v. 28, 31,37). God allows us to go through the worst in order to bring out our best!

G - GO THE EXTRA MILE

Jesus modeled this on the Mount of Olives through His teaching found in Matthew 5. Watch this, "Whoever compels you to go one mile, go with him two" (v. 41). "Love your enemies and bless them who curse you" (v. 44). If you live by these principles, you will not blend in; you will definitely stand out!

You will not be remembered for doing things you were expected to do. But when you go the extra mile by doing what is not expected, you will stand out. One thing is certain, there are not traffic jams on the extra mile!

E - ENTHUSIASM

Dale Carnegie once said, "Cash can buy, but it takes enthusiasm to sell." That's good. A great example of this can be read in 1 Kings 10. The queen of Sheba went to Solomon's temple as a critic, to find fault, but notice what she said after she got there: *"Happy* are your men, and *happy* are these your servants" (v. 8). Of all the splendor of Solomon's temple, it was the enthusiasm of Solomon's men and servants that stood out.

The word "enthusiasm" comes from the Greek *en Theos* which means "with God." Hey leader, enthusiasm is an inside work. It's a result of spending time with Jesus. Do you want to stand out? Be enthusiastic! Nothing is as contagious as enthusiasm.

We are called to stand out and not blend in. Remember: **It's not *what* you do that sets you apart, it's *how* you do what you are called to do.** If you want to be an effective leader, retreat to advance, spend time with Jesus, and keep your cutting edge sharp!

IGNITORS

- Have you noticed some dullness to your edge?

- Has average performance been acceptable? Good enough?

- Do you ever feel the need to retreat to advance?

NOTES

LEADERS WHO STAND OUT!

> He who leads and no one follows ... only takes a walk.
>
> JOHN MAXWELL

IF THIS DESCRIBES your leadership status, I've come by to remind you, **this is only your starting place.** Just don't allow this to become your *resting* place. When you have the title of "leader" and not many followers, that spells F-R-U-S-T-R-A-T-I-O-N. Don't let that intimidate you. Let it motivate you to make a change. **Frustration could be an indication that God wants to change something in your life**! People will join you because of *vision*, and people will leave you because of *leadership*.

What a joy it has been for me to share with you these ten proven principles that work. However, no principle will work unless you do it. God's PRINCIPLES plus your PERSPIRATION equals great POSSIBILITIES. Remember, there are stand-out leaders in the Bible who have stand-out qualities that can make you a stand-out leader.

INITIATIVE

A powerful leadership gem to learn and to live by is **get to it and stick to it**! You have heard it said, "If you want to get a job done, give it to a busy man." This saying is a perfect description of Moses. In the book of Numbers, Moses had the responsibility in leading a troublesome group of people, who even tried God's patience, through the wilderness to the Promised Land. The people complained about their accommodations, the free food God provided for them to eat, and their lack of water. Moses had his hands full. God then asked Moses "on the first day of the second month, in the second year after they had come out of the land of Egypt" to take a census of all Israel (Numbers 1:1).

Let's assume that Moses is just like us. What would your reaction be? "Count everybody? God, You know that my hands are full taking care of the natural and spiritual welfare of all these people. To top it off, I'm writing the Bible!" Rather than complain, notice what Moses did. Scripture tells us, "On the first day of the second month ... as the Lord commanded Moses, so he numbered them" (v. 17-18). Did you see that? On the same day that Moses was given his assignment from God, he did it. **You create opportunities by performing, not complaining**. Waiting to get started only invites distraction and broken focus. Broken focus is a leading cause in leadership failure. **Never confuse activity for accomplishment.**

WHOLEHEARTEDNESS

Hezekiah, son of King Ahaz, became king when he was 25 years old. Seeing his father's wickedness, Hezekiah wanted no part of it. He wanted to make a positive impact in the lives of the people he was leading. In a very short time, Hezekiah's leadership caused a total turn around: "So there was great joy in Jerusalem for since the time of Solomon ... there had been nothing like this in Jerusalem" (2 Chronicles 30:26).

What caused this turn around? "In every work that he began in the service of the house of God ... he did it with *all his heart*. So he prospered" (2 Chronicles 31:21). It was not only *what* but *how* Hezekiah did things that made an impact. Paul wrote, "Whatever you do, do it *heartily*, as unto the Lord" (Colossians 3:23). Leaders cannot afford to have their heart massaged with statements such as, "Take it easy" or "Don't overdo it" and "Don't work too hard." These statements can lead to mediocrity. When working for the Lord, good enough never is!

SINGLE MINDEDNESS

"If you chase two rabbits, both will escape." Paul wrote, *"One thing* I do, forgetting those things which are behind and reaching forward to those things which are ahead" (Philippians 3:13). When you focus on your God-call, you eliminate wrong options. Wrongs options could be things from your past. **Your past is a point of reference, not a place of residence**.

God is ready to do news things in new ways. The biggest enemy to the new things that God wants to do in you are the old things. Watch this, "Do not remember the former things, nor consider the things of old. Behold, I will do a *new thing"* (Isaiah 43:18-19). Time and time again we are told to look out the windshield and stop looking through the rearview mirror. **In your search for that which is new, be careful not to forsake that which is true**.

Lately I've noticed an increase of leadership notes and quotes on social media. I believe that God is calling the Church to light a candle instead of cursing the darkness. Leader, it's time to strengthen the leadership qualities that God has placed inside of you. My sincere prayer is that these proven principles that have made an impact in my life and ministry have awakened the leader inside of you.

Pastor Gary

ABOUT THE AUTHOR

Gary L. Tustin was born and raised in Latrobe, Pennsylvania. In 1967, he accepted the call and entered the ministry. For over 50 years, Pastor Gary has been committed to the pastoral ministry which has taken him to Arkansas, Florida, Tennessee, and Pennsylvania.

Pastor Gary is the Founding Pastor of the Greater Johnstown Christian Fellowship (GJCF). His heart is to develop younger leaders into realizing their full potential in Christ as the next generation leads the Church into the future.

Pastor Gary and his wife Peggy reside in Johnstown, Pennsylvania. He is the father of two children—his daughter, Lori, and son, Brian. Pastor Gary is also a grandfather of five: Alyssa, Luke, Olivia, Brianna and Trevor. He is also a great-grandfather to Judah.

facebook.com/gary.tustin.1